Cooking for Children

What Children Like to Eat

> Author: **Dagmar von Cramm** | Photos: **Michael Brauner**

Contents

The Recipes

Appendix

Cooking for and Eating with Children

Your child has now joined you at the family table. They're constantly getting to know new smells, tastes, and preparations. Their eating behavior is being shaped. Whatever they learn now about eating and drinking will accompany them throughout their life. From ages 1 to 7, it's not a matter of preparing special children's foods; it's all relevant. Cooking for children is not just a means to an end, but an opportunity to promote the development of their minds and skills, experience togetherness, and help them understand the world.

What Your Child Needs

During the early years, you can give your child a foundation of healthy nutrition and good eating habits. At age one, your child tolerates pretty much everything adults eat, although with less seasoning, well-done, cut into small pieces, and not too dry. After their incisors appear, they start to get molars and their digestive systems are ready to engage life. In no way do toddlers—much less children of kindergarten age—require specially prepared diets. Children this age are no longer as susceptible to germs; normal household hygiene is sufficient.

> **1** *Fresh fruit, vegetables, and yogurt make ideal snacks.*

IMPORTANT It's not so easy to wean children from a bottle. For the sake of their teeth, however, the bottle should disappear by their second birthday.

What's the Situation?

➤ Children tend to take in more calories than they need.

➤ They eat too much fat, primarily "hidden" animal fat in hotdogs, cheese, fast food, sweets, and snack foods, thus increasing the risk of arteriosclerosis.

➤ Children eat more protein than they need. This is usually linked to fat (e.g., cheese, meat, hot dogs). Experts disagree about whether this is harmful.

➤ Children eat too little grain, potatoes, vegetables and fruit: Forty-two percent eat almost no fruit and one-third will only seldom eat vegetables.

➤ At the same time, they eat too much sugar and white flour.

➤ Children drink too little, and when they do drink, it's too often sweetened soft drinks that give them a boost of energy but have no nutritional value.

➤ Foods enriched with vitamins and minerals give children lots of these substances in unmeasured doses. We don't yet know if this does any good.

➤ Afternoons and evenings, children eat too many sweets, which don't supply enough valuable nutrients.

NOTE The weak point in our children's menu plan is the between-meal snacking.

What You Can Do

Here's basically how the food plan should look to provide a balanced ratio of nutrients (50–55 percent of food energy from carbohydrates, 30–35 percent from fat, and 15 percent from protein):
Minimize: Fatty, salty, and high-sugar foods such as fast food, fried food and confectionery, and baked goods.

In moderation: Animal foods such as milk, fish, meat, eggs, and seafood once a week as a source of iodine. **Maximize:** Plant foods such as vegetables, lettuce, fruit, potatoes, grain products (preferably whole grain), and beverages such as water, tea, and sparkling fruit juices.

Children do best if they get three main meals a day and two snacks, but don't let this become an invitation to constant munching. Even toddlers can manage a trip to the playground without a picnic.

How Much Your Child Should Weigh

Girls Age	BMI (normal range)	Boys Age	BMI (normal range)
1 year	14.8–18.3	1 year	15.2–18.7
2 years	14.3–17.9	2 years	14.6–18.0
3 years	13.9–17.6	3 years	14.1–17.6
4 years	13.7–17.5	4 years	13.9–17.5
5 years	13.6–17.7	5 years	13.8–17.6
6 years	13.7–18.0	6 years	13.8–17.9
7 years	13.7–18.5	7 years	13.9–18.3

BMI table: This table shows the normal range. Children whose BMI is below the normal range are underweight and those above it are overweight. If your child weighs too much, he or she doesn't need to lose weight, but should stay at the same weight until growth restores the balance.

Too Little	Remedy
Fiber	Fruit, vegetables, whole grains
Iodine	Seafood, iodized salt
Iron	Red meat, millet
Zinc	Meat
Calcium	Milk and dairy products
Folic acid	Raw fruit and vegetables
Liquid	Water

Is My Child's Weight Correct?

This is difficult to judge. Just before a growth spurt, children often become a little pudgy and then wiry afterward. These growth phases are taken into account in our table, including the differences between boys and girls. First you have to calculate your child's body mass index. This is weight in pounds divided by height in meters squared.

Example: Your daughter weighs 37 pounds, is 3'5" tall, and is 4 years old. Calculate the BMI as follows: Weight in pounds divided by height in inches squared, times 703. **For example:** BMI = 37 (weight in pounds) divided by 1681 (height in inches squared: 41 x 41) = 0.022 x 703 = 15.4. This is fine for a 4 year old girl.

What Children Like to Eat

Unfortunately, children don't always have an instinctive preference for what's good for them. Our lives and foods have wandered too far from their roots, assuming we ever had this instinct in the first place. The problem of "unhealthy cravings" and imbalance are certainly not easy to solve, but if you know your child's nature and preferences, you can deal with it better: Even babies like sweet things, as do older children, and they don't like bitter and strong flavors.

Children love simple foods. They like to eat what they know.

1 *Children like eating best with company.*

Children are smarter and more sensible than adults. They experience eating on all levels: Hearing, sight, taste, smell, and touch. In addition to the flavor, mouth-feel is also important. If it crunches, crackles, or goes down smoothly, children love it. The most important influence is the example of the parents (and according to studies, especially of the mother) and, as children grow, that of their friends. Your dislikes have a bigger impact than your likes.

Eating Right

The more often a child tries a dish, the higher the chances that they'll like it. Keep letting your child try dishes that they don't like or don't know. If they don't like it, they don't have to eat it. Don't avoid every little conflict. With persistence, you may eventually wear them down. The only way your child can develop a taste for a dish is if they get repeated chances to try it.

But it isn't just a matter of what they eat. How they eat also plays an important role. To deal with life, children need routines and rules. This includes fixed, reliable meal times: Breakfast, lunch, dinner, and a morning and afternoon snack consisting of dairy products, cut-up fruit, or a low-fat, low-sugar pastry. But don't allow your child unrestricted access to the refrigerator and pantry. Try to maintain periods of fasting. For example, before common meals, your child should at most nibble on a carrot to keep from spoiling their appetite. Hunger and fullness are important body signals that your child should learn to recognize. They can handle waiting until they're hungry to eat. After all, hunger is the best spice!

The Environment Teaches, Too

During the early years, you as parents are still lords of the kitchen and dining room. But the first uprisings can already start in the supermarket. Advertising aimed at children falls on fertile soil and your children want to eat what they see on TV or hear about on the radio. What should you do? Don't allow yourself to be blackmailed, but don't completely banish them from this flashy, colorful world, either. Once in a while, try something with a critical eye—best done in moderation and at the proper time.

In Kindergarten

As active parents, you can help shape the rules at kindergarten. Make the teachers your allies, lend a hand, and establish solidarity with the other parents.

Sensible, proven rules for kindergarten life:
➤ An organized second breakfast is better than having children simply eat when they're hungry. Hungry kids who had to get up extra early can have their first breakfast at a table.
➤ For meals, the children should sit at a table and no one should sit alone.
➤ Limit drinks to water and home-brewed fruit tea. If a refrigerator is available, you can also give them milk or chocolate milk for breakfast.
➤ Kindergarten should be declared a sugar-free zone.
➤ Avoid prepackaged snacks.

2 *Give your child a sandwich and fruit to take to kindergarten.*

Cooking, baking, planting, and harvesting are ideal subjects for the kindergarten years. You'll be astonished what your children will eat in the company of their contemporaries. If your child attends daycare, food plays an even greater role in their care, because they're also being served lunch. Again, parents should be significantly involved. Exercise your rights, for example in the Parent Teacher's Association (PTA), and take your influence seriously so your child can receive a healthy, nutritious, and child-appropriate lunch.

Children and Cooking

With the first birthday, your child is a full, though small, participant at the family table. They no longer need special treatment. What they do need is healthy family care. The wonderful thing about this is that you can kill many birds with one stone. Regular, shared meals and sensible eating rules also promote the parents' nutrition, help establish commonalities, and develop a family conversation. Naturally, your child cannot yet speak, but they already understand much more than you give them credit for and grow into the family rituals and rules from the very start. For this reason, you should consciously plan at least one common meal each day. Although we used to experience the extremely strict structures of our own childhoods as a burden of family life, we now see their necessity. It isn't until you have to make an appointment for every meal that eating in the family circle becomes a rare and valued effort.

Everyday Rules

Provide structures: Important basic rules include no snacks for an hour before meals except for raw fruit or vegetables, and start and end meals at the same time. For the duration of the meal, put aside the newspaper and turn off the TV, radio, and cell phone. Even toddlers can demonstrate or learn good behavior within their capacities. If they throw their spoon or stick their hands in the salad, intervene.

Kitchen as Playground

There's nothing like working around the house and garden to give small children an introduction to life. This is where the old rules of demonstration and imitation apply. You can help your child learn to handle spoons, knives, bowls, and pots. Housework is a good time for questions and answers, songs and rhymes, and sometimes even for cuddling. Certainly, you're often pressed for time and become inpatient. It's better to give yourself more time so you'll have extra to spare for a leisure activity. Making cookies or stirring salad dressing is as stimulating for your child as a playgroup. Creative, active exposure to food, eating and drinking promotes cognitive and motor skills, develops your child's sense of taste, and teaches them the value of food and drink. The time you expend on common meals will benefit the whole family.

> **1** *Let your children decorate their own birthday cupcakes.*

Celebrating with Children

Celebrations always involve eating and drinking, starting with Christmas cookies and ending with Easter eggs. By celebrating holidays, you create traditions that will stay with your children throughout their lives and give them a sense of security. But keep in mind that whatever you introduce will be hard to change later on, because children are very conservative.

The First Party

A child's birthday is the most important day in their year and it must, of course, be celebrated. Your child won't get much out of the first birthday, so enjoy it for your own sake. The second and third birthdays are still happily celebrated within the family. It isn't until children enter kindergarten that friends come into the picture. Rule of thumb: Invite the same number of guests as your child's age. Stick to a familiar group and play tried-

and-true games. As a rule, the best foods are dry cakes, muffins, and simple sandwiches. If you serve cut-up fruit instead of sweets and chilled cucumber slices instead of chips, you're sure to have happy parents and hopefully happy little guests. Have a lot of beverages on hand—running around makes kids thirsty.

Keep the following basic rules in mind when planning a party:
➤ Food doesn't always have to be sweet. Pretzels and pizza

are also favorites.
➤ Arrange the food on a buffet. Children should be able to eat everything with their hands.
➤ Bottled water, fruit tea, and sparkling juices help avoid stomach aches, diarrhea, and unnecessary frenzy.
➤ First let the children play, then eat, and then play again.
➤ Let your children participate in the planning. They know best what will work and be fun for their friends. You don't have to provide children's entertainment like in fast food restaurants.

What Can My Child Do?

Drinking

As of 1 year, your child can...
...drink from a safety cup with help.

As of 1½ years, your child can...
...drink from a safety cup alone.

As of 2 years, your child can...
...drink from a cup.

As of 3 years, your child can...
...drink with a straw.

As of 4 years, your child can...
...drink from a glass.

As of 5 years, your child can...
...pour their own drink.

As of 6 years, your child can...
...drink from a glass.

Eating

As of 1 year, your child can...
...hold a spoon but not manipulate it alone.

As of 1½ years, your child can...
..."play eating" with a spoon.

As of 2 years, your child can...
...eat with a spoon, but not without spilling.

As of 3 years, your child can...
...eat safely with a spoon or fork and a food pusher.

As of 4 years, your child can...
...cut soft foods and spread butter on bread.

As of 5 years, your child can...
...cut harder foods (e.g., bread, meat).

As of 6 years, your child can...
...safely handle a knife and fork.

Playing

As of 1 year, your child can...

...play with pots, lids, spoons, etc.

As of 1½ years, your child can...

...stir, put things in cabinets, and take them out.

As of 2 years, your child can...

..."play cooking."

As of 3 years, your child can...

...suggest food, smell, taste, and try to cook with you.

As of 4 years, your child can...

...cook for dolls on a doll's stove.

As of 5 years, your child can...

...play cooking and baking with friends and set the table.

As of 6 years, your child can...

...cook "real food" and play restaurant.

Helping

As of 1 year, your child can...

...not really help.

As of 1½ years, your child can...

...get small things for you and try to help.

As of 2 years, your child can...

...sort food, stir yogurts and pick fruit, vegetables, and herbs in the garden.

As of 3 years, your child can...

...rinse fruit, vegetables and lettuce, and stir batter.

As of 4 years, your child can...

...arrange lunchmeat and cheese on a plate, stand at the stove and help cook, peel and cut up ingredients, and stir sauces.

As of 5 years, your child can...

...set and clear the table, help bake a cake, and beat eggs.

As of 6 years, your child can...

...fry eggs in a pan, shop for small items, weigh and measure ingredients, and cook small dishes by themselves.

What Do I Do If My Child...

...Won't Eat Vegetables?

It's worth exposing children to vegetables, primarily because vegetables are incredible sources of nutrients that are essential for healthy growth. Often children would rather eat vegetables such as carrots, kohlrabi, cucumbers, bell peppers, and tomatoes raw as snacks. Serve them with a dip. They're also more acceptable to children puréed in sauces or soups. Make vegetable juice in a juicer and mix it with fruit juice. Don't give up—vegetables strengthen the immune system and prevent obesity! Here again, the example of the parents is extremely important!

> **1** Occasional sweets are okay, but only in small amounts and moderation.

...Won't Give up the Bottle?

Don't let your child reach for the bottle any time they want as a replacement for a pacifier. Some time during their second year, the cup will start to replace the bottle more and more, although it may be difficult at the beginning. Start by keeping your child's bottle out of sight during the day and consistently offer them drinks in cups. In the evening and possibly in the morning, you can still allow them their bottle, but you must retire it completely at the end of their second year, and take away the pacifier at three. You might take advantage of a vacation to initiate a bottle-free time. Or let your child say a formal goodbye to the bottle and inaugurate a "favorite cup." Some children give up the bottle on their own, while others need a push. Do this very consciously. The longer you wait, the harder and more painful it will be for your child.

...Always Wants Sweets?

Sugar damages teeth and displaces valuable foods in the menu. It is consumed unconsciously in sweetened drinks and is combined with a lot of fat in chocolate, etc. A sensible plan is to limit sugar consumption to no more than 10 percent of daily calories. As long as your child is at home and doesn't have older siblings, you can avoid the temptation of sweets. Just don't buy any. But eventually, the sweet environment will pull them in! The important thing is to prevent the establishment of sweet habits. Don't console your child with sweets, not even when they're upset. As a snack, offer your child fruit yogurt and cut-up fruit. Once in a while, prepare a sweet main dish (see pages 48–55) or a dessert. Establish a "treasure chest" where your child can accumulate candy and let them choose one treat a day after a meal.

...Plays with His or Her Food?

Playing means learning. But naturally there are limits, depending on age. Once in a while, serve finger food and let your child help you cook so they can satisfy their desire to play and experience food with all their senses. If your child eats with you at the table and touches it with their hands, slurps and slobbers in their bowl, intervene, but don't spoil your child's enjoyment of eating by laying down too many restrictions. Let them stir the pot, mash the potatoes on their plate, and spread their own butter. It might be a little hard on your nerves in the beginning, but you'll be rewarded later on by greater independence, both for you and your child. However, when an obviously full child keeps playing with their food to the point of making it inedible, it's time to put a stop to it. This is when you have to make it absolutely clear to your child that their behavior is ruining the appetite of the others at the table.

...Is Always Hungry Between Meals?

Your child won't starve if they go a couple hours without eating! A second, mid-morning breakfast and a little something in the afternoon in addition to the main meals is all children need. Snacking, on the other hand, causes problems, since it usually involves unhealthy foods like chips, candy, and fast food. Try to establish clear boundaries around eating. Eating should be done at the table and, if possible, in company. Don't allow snacks before a meal. If they're really hungry, you can just as easily give children raw vegetables or fresh fruit.

....Won't Try Anything New?

Often children under three years of age love to experiment and don't start refusing until kindergarten. Reliable rules often help. If they try a spoonful and decide they don't like it, they don't have to eat it. Don't be discouraged by their refusal. Keep trying.

> **2** *Water with raspberries and lime slices are very delicious and refreshing.*

Avoid any power struggles, especially before they turn three!

...Never Cleans Their Plate?

Today, most children aren't expected to clean their plates. It is important, however, that they learn to correctly assess their own hunger. Serving themselves is already important for kindergarten-age children. It's better for them to take several servings than start out by piling on too much. If they always leave food on the plate, heat it up and serve it to them at the next meal.

13

For Breakfast and Dinner

Even a cold meal can fortify your child. Milk drinks for morning grumps, granola and fruit for "cereal fans," and healthy whole grain breads with low-sugar spreads provide a delicious variety and are ready in a jiffy. Dips and salads make excellent accompaniments to fresh bread.

Quick Recipes

Fruit Tea

SERVES 2

➤ 1 tsp rosehip tea (or 1 rosehip teabag) | 1 tsp dried chopped apple | 1 tsp raisins | 1 tsp flaked coconut | 1 dash apple juice

1 | Place rosehip tea, dried apple, raisins, and coconut in a tea net or ball.

2 | Bring 1¾ cups water to a boil and pour into a teapot. Add tea mixture. Cover and let steep for 10 minutes and then remove the tea. Sweeten with apple juice and serve hot.

➤ Variation: For homemade iced tea, combine 4 cups fruit tea with the juice of 1 lemon, sweeten to taste with a little sugar, and serve ice cold.

Vitamin C Boost

SERVES 2

➤ 2 kiwis | 1 dash apple juice | 1 cup cranberry juice | Ice cubes | 1 lemon for garnish (optional)

1 | Peel kiwis, rinse under cold water, and purée with apple juice in a blender.

2 | Place ice cubes in 2 glasses. First pour in kiwi purée and then carefully pour on cranberry nectar to create 2 layers. Serve with a straw. If desired, garnish with 1 lemon slice.

Rich in Minerals
Date Chocolate Drink

SERVES 2
- ➤ 4 dried dates
  1¼ cups milk
  1 tsp cocoa powder
  Grated chocolate
  for garnish

🕐 Prep time: 10 minutes

1 | Remove pits from dates and finely chop. In a saucepan, heat milk, add cocoa and dates, and bring to a boil.

2 | Remove pan from heat. Pour milk mixture into a blender and purée until the date pieces have almost disappeared. Pour into 2 glasses and sprinkle with grated chocolate. Serve hot.

NOTE Dates are very rich in minerals. They are a natural way to make the chocolate mixture creamy and sweet. Their flavor is very compatible with cocoa.

Fast
Berry Yogurt Smoothie

SERVES 2
- ➤ ¾ cup fresh or frozen mixed berries
  2 tbs sugar
  ¼ tsp vanilla
  1 cup plain yogurt
  ½ cup cold milk

🕐 Prep time: 10 minutes

1 | Rinse and sort berries. Set aside several berries for garnish. Sprinkle berries with sugar and let stand briefly.

2 | Combine yogurt, milk and prepared berries in a blender, and purée until smooth. Pour into 2 glasses, garnish with reserved berries, and serve immediately.

- ➤ Variation: Prepare yogurt drinks with other fruits depending on personal preferences and the season. Great served with fresh, ripe bananas, apricots, mangos, or honeydew melons.

Rich in Calcium
Latte Bambino

SERVES 2
- ➤ 4 tsp instant decaffeinated coffee
  2 tsp brown sugar
  1¾ cups milk

🕐 Prep time: 10 minutes

1 | In each glass, combine 2 tsp coffee beverage granules and 1 tsp sugar and mix well. Bring ½ cup water to a boil and pour into glasses. Stir until mixture is dissolved.

2 | Heat milk but don't boil. Beat milk with a wire whisk until foamy. Carefully spoon foamed milk into coffee beverage.

NOTE Cold, non-fat or low-fat milk foams better than whole milk.

Rich in Calcium

Fruity Yogurt Cream

SERVES 4

➤ 1 ripe banana
2 tbs lemon juice
1 cup low-fat sour cream
$2/3$ cup plain yogurt
1 ripe mango
3 tbs flaked
coconut, toasted

🕐 Prep time: 20 minutes

1 | Purée banana and lemon juice in a blender. Blend in sour cream and yogurt until smooth. Refrigerate for 2 hours.

2 | Before serving, peel mango, cut the fruit from the pit, dice finely, and fold into the yogurt mixture.

3 | Spoon yogurt cream into dishes and sprinkle with grated coconut.

➤ Variation: Replace mango with other fruits. Instead of grated coconut, use grated chocolate or nuts.

For the Pantry

Chocolate Granola

MAKES 20–25 SERVINGS

➤ $1\frac{1}{2}$ cups unpopped popcorn (or 10–12 cups popped corn)
$7\frac{1}{2}$ cups multigrain flakes
1 cup chopped hazelnuts
$3/4$ cup sunflower seeds
$2/3$ cup raisins
$2/3$ cup banana chips
$1/2$ cup wheat germ
$1/3$ cup dried chopped dates
3 tbs grated semi-sweet chocolate or chocolate chips
2 tbs cocoa powder
1 tsp cinnamon

🕐 Prep time: 20 minutes

1 | Use popped popcorn or heat a large, ungreased pan with a lid. Add popcorn, cover, and heat until the corn pops. Shake the pan back and forth. Let the popcorn cool.

2 | Meanwhile, thoroughly mix all the other ingredients in a large bowl. Add popcorn at the end and stir. Transfer granola to storage containers. If well sealed, it will keep for several weeks.

Nutritious

Power Breakfast

SERVES 2

➤ $1/4$ cup rolled oats or wheat
1 cup plain yogurt
2 tsp concentrated agave juice or honey
1 apple
2 tbs walnuts, toasted
8 strawberries (or 1 orange)

🕐 Prep time: 20 minutes

1 | Grind oats or wheat medium-fine in a small food processor or coffee grinder. Mix with $1/4$ cup water to make a porridge, cover, and refrigerate overnight.

2 | The next morning, combine porridge with yogurt and agave juice or honey. Rinse and peel apple, and stir in.

3 | Rinse strawberries and finely chop, or, if using an orange, peel and cut into small pieces. Sprinkle granola with walnuts and garnish with fruit.

For the Pantry | Inexpensive

Vegetarian Lentil Spread

MAKES ABOUT 1¼ CUPS SPREAD

➤ 1 cup tomato juice
⅔ cup red lentils
1 small yellow bell pepper
Salt
Freshly ground pepper
Basil

1 | Bring tomato juice to a boil. Add lentils and simmer over low heat for 5–10 minutes or until softened, then purée.

2 | Finely chop bell pepper in a food processor. Stir bell pepper into lentil mixture and season to taste with salt, pepper, and basil. Transfer spread to a covered container and store in the refrigerator. Keeps for about 5 days.

For the Pantry | Flavorful

Spelt Spread

MAKES ABOUT 2 CUPS SPREAD

➤ ¾ lb fresh mushrooms
1 onion
1 clove garlic
2 tbs oil
⅔ cup vegetable stock
⅔ cup cracked spelt
1½ tsp each of dried marjoram and thyme
Salt
Pepper

1 | Peel onion and garlic and finely dice. Clean mushrooms and slice thinly. Heat oil and brown mushrooms, onion, and garlic. Add stock, bring to a boil. Add spelt and herbs and let stand for 10 minutes.

2 | Purée all ingredients and season to taste with salt and pepper. Transfer to a covered container and store in the refrigerator. Keeps for about 5 days.

For the Pantry | Fruity

Raspberry Almond Paste

MAKES ABOUT ³/₄ CUP SPREAD

➤ 1 packet unflavored gelatin
  (about 2 tbs)

2 tbs granulated sugar

1 cup fresh raspberries (may
substitute frozen, thawed)

1 tbs honey

¹/₂ cup slivered almonds

1 | Combine gelatin, sugar, and ¹/₂ cup boiling water. Stir and let stand until gelatin is dissolved, about 5 minutes.

2 | Rinse raspberries carefully. Combine with honey and gelatin mixture and purée in a blender at the highest setting for 10 minutes until the mixture starts to gel.

3 | In an ungreased pan, toast slivered almonds and stir into raspberry mixture. Transfer raspberry paste to a sterilized jelly jar and let cool. Keeps for about 7 days.

For the Pantry | Low-Fat

Raisin Chocolate Cream

MAKES ABOUT 1 CUP SPREAD

➤ 1 cup apple juice

¹/₃ cup raisins

¹/₄ cup bulgur wheat

4¹/₂ cups ground hazelnuts

1 tbs cocoa powder

1 | Combine apple juice, raisins and bulgur in a small saucepan, and bring to a boil. Simmer over low heat for 20–25 minutes until thickened.

2 | Meanwhile, toast hazelnuts in an ungreased pan. Add nuts and cocoa powder to bulgur-raisin mixture and purée in food processor until nearly smooth. Transfer to a covered container and let cool. Keeps refrigerated for about 7 days.

Non-Dairy and Egg-Free
Tomato Red Pepper Dip

SERVES 4

➤ 2 ripe tomatoes
2 red bell peppers
1 small onion
1 tbs olive oil
½ bunch parsley
2 tbs tomato paste
Freshly ground pepper
Salt
1 pinch sugar

🕐 Prep time: 20 minutes

1 | Finely chop tomatoes, bell peppers, and onion. In a small pan, heat 1 tbs oil and braise tomatoes, bell peppers, and onion for 2–3 minutes. Remove pan from heat.

2 | Rinse parsley, shake dry, remove leaves from stems, and finely chop. Combine tomato paste, cooked vegetables, and parsley. Season to taste with salt, pepper, and sugar.

Non-Dairy and Egg-Free
Guacamole

SERVES 4

➤ 1 lime
2 ripe avocados
1 small clove garlic, minced or pressed
½ bunch Italian parsley
Salt
Freshly ground pepper

🕐 Prep time: 15 minutes

1 | Grate lime peel and squeeze juice. Cut avocados in half, remove pits, peel, and coarsely chop. Combine avocado immediately with lime juice.

2 | Rinse parsley, shake dry, and finely chop leaves. Combine lime peel, garlic, parsley, and avocado. Purée or hand mash until nearly smooth. Season to taste with salt and pepper.

➤ Delicious with boiled or baked potatoes, grilled foods, or as a bread spread.

Classic
Chive dip

SERVES 4

➤ 2 bunches parsley
2 cups sour cream or whole milk yogurt
1 clove garlic, minced or pressed
Salt
Freshly ground pepper

🕐 Prep time: 15 minutes

1 | Rinse chives, shake dry, and finely chop.

2 | Combine sour cream or yogurt and garlic. Season with salt and pepper. Just before serving, fold in chives.

➤ Delicious as a spread on bread, as vegetable dip, and on potatoes.

➤ Variation: Use other herbs. Stir in grated carrots, diced radishes, bell peppers, tomatoes or cucumbers, or 1 small, diced hard-boiled egg and a little mustard, toasted nuts, or seeds.

Inexpensive
Raw Carrot Corn Salad

SERVES 4

- ➤ 1 lb carrots
- 1 tart apple
- $1/3$ cup yogurt
- $1/4$ cup sour cream
- 1 tsp mild mustard
- 2 tbs oil
- 2 tbs orange juice
- Salt
- Freshly ground pepper
- Sugar
- $3/4$ cup fresh or frozen thawed corn kernels

🕐 Prep time: 30 minutes

1 | Rinse carrots, clean, and peel. Rinse apple, cut into quarters, and remove core. Finely grate carrots and apple.

2 | Combine yogurt, sour cream, mustard, oil and orange juice, and mix until smooth. Season to taste with salt, pepper, and sugar.

3 | Mix carrots and apple with dressing. Add corn and refrigerate for 30 minutes before serving.

Sophisticated | Mediterranean
Couscous Salad

SERVES 4

- ➤ 1 large lemon
- 5 tbs olive oil
- Salt
- Freshly ground pepper
- 1 cup, plus 2 tbs uncooked couscous
- 1 bunch green onions
- 3 tomatoes
- $1/2$ cucumber
- 1 bunch parsley
- $1/2$ cup chopped black olives
- 1 clove garlic, pressed
- 5 oz feta cheese, crumbled

🕐 Prep time: 30 minutes

1 | Grate lemon peel and squeeze juice. Combine $1/4$ cup lemon juice, $1 2/3$ cups hot water, oil, lemon peel, salt, and pepper. Add couscous and let stand for 15 minutes or until liquid has been absorbed. (Or, if purchasing couscous in a package, please follow directions on package.)

2 | Rinse, clean, and finely chop vegetables and parsley.

3 | Combine couscous, vegetables, parsley, olives, and garlic. Stir in feta and season to taste with salt and pepper. Serve at room temperature or cold.

For the Pantry
Lemon-Mustard Dressing

SERVES 4

- ➤ 1 lemon
- $3/4$ cup canola oil
- 1 tsp mild mustard
- Salt
- Freshly ground pepper
- Sugar

🕐 Prep time: 10 minutes

1 | Grate zest and squeeze juice from lemon.

2 | Combine lemon juice, zest, mustard, oil, and 6 tbs water in a screw-top jar. Seal jar well and shake until the ingredients are well mixed.

3 | Season generously with salt, pepper, and sugar. Keeps in the refrigerator for about 1 week.

- ➤ Goes with all green salads and potato salad.

Combinables

Children love orderly arrangements on their plate! Here you'll find fantastic sauces with new side dishes from polenta to bulgur. They can all be combined with other things, including noodles. How about a Veggie Burger or Meatloaf Muffin instead of the same old hot dog?

Quick Recipes

Meatloaf Muffins

MAKES 12 MUFFINS

➤ 1 slice stale bread | 1 small onion |
1 clove garlic | 1 small red bell pepper |
$\frac{1}{2}$ lb lean, ground beef | 1 egg | 2 tbs
low-fat sour cream | Bread crumbs |
Salt | Cayenne pepper | Paprika |
Grease for the muffin pan

1 | Preheat oven to 400°F. Soften bread
in warm water. Peel onion and garlic
and finely dice. Finely dice bell pepper.
Grease a muffin pan.

2 | Squeeze out bread and knead together
with ground meat, bell pepper, egg, sour
cream, onion, and garlic. If necessary,
knead in bread crumbs to make mixture
firm enough to hold together. Season
mixture with salt, cayenne, and paprika.
Divide evenly into muffin cups. Bake in
the oven for 15–20 minutes.

Veggie Burger

MAKES 12 BURGERS

➤ 6–7 slices stale bread | 1 small red
bell pepper | 2 eggs | Salt | Pepper |
Nutmeg | Paprika | $\frac{2}{3}$ cup low-fat
ricotta cheese | $\frac{1}{2}$ cup corn kernels |
3 tbs chopped chives | 6 tbs oat flakes |
Oil for frying

1 | Dice bread and bell pepper. Whisk
together eggs, salt, pepper, nutmeg, and
paprika. Pour over bread and let stand for
5 minutes. Knead in ricotta, vegetables,
and chives. If the mixture is too soft, add
oat flakes until mixture is firm enough to
handle. Shape into burgers and coat with
additional oat flakes.

2 | In a nonstick pan, heat oil and fry
burgers on both sides until golden-brown.

Fast | Inexpensive
Cauliflower Curry

SERVES 4

➤ 1 small cauliflower
1 onion
1 tbs butter
1 cup vegetable stock
¼ cup milk
1 tsp mild curry powder
1 tsp sugar
2 tbs crème fraîche
Salt
Freshly ground pepper
2 uncooked bratwursts
Cooked basmati rice
Chopped parsley

🕑 Prep time: 50 minutes

1 | Rinse cauliflower and divide into florets. Peel onion and finely dice. In a saucepan, heat butter and braise onion until translucent.

2 | Add cauliflower to the onions. Pour in vegetable stock and milk. Stir in curry and sugar. Bring to a boil, cover, and simmer for 15 minutes until the cauliflower is done.

3 | Remove saucepan from heat. Remove about half the cauliflower and set aside. Add crème fraîche to remaining cauliflower and purée until smooth. Season to taste with salt and pepper.

4 | Slice bratwurst into ½-inch thick pieces. Heat sauce and gently cook bratwurst in the sauce over low heat for 5 minutes. Arrange sauce with sausage and reserved cauliflower over basmati rice mixed with chopped parsley.

Rich in Carotene | Inexpensive
Polenta Slices

SERVES 4

➤ For the slices:
1 cup milk
1 tsp salt
1½ cups uncooked polenta
3 tbs oil for frying
➤ For the sauce:
5–6 oz fresh celery root
1 tsp oil
3 tbs tomato paste
1 can tomatoes (28 oz)
2 tsp dried oregano
Salt
Pepper
1 tsp sugar
Soy sauce

🕑 Prep time: 50 minutes

1 | In a nonstick pan, combine 2 cups water, milk and salt, and bring to a boil. Stir in polenta and simmer over low heat while stirring constantly until it thickens. Remove from heat. Wet a knife blade and smooth the surface of the polenta in the pan. Let cool for 30 minutes.

2 | Meanwhile, make the sauce: Rinse celery root, peel, and finely grate. Heat oil and braise celery root for 2–3 minutes. Add tomato paste and brown briefly. Add tomatoes and oregano and simmer for 10 minutes. Purée then reduce for another 5 minutes. Season to taste with salt, pepper, sugar, and a little soy sauce.

3 | Cut polenta into slices and remove from pan. Clean the pan, heat oil, and fry polenta slices on both sides until golden-brown. Serve with tomato sauce.

Fast | Easy
Vegetable Sauce with Couscous

SERVES 4

➤ 2 tsp butter
2 tsp flour
1 onion
2 carrots
1 zucchini
1 tsp oil
2 cups vegetable juice
Salt
Freshly ground pepper
2 tbs chopped parsley
2 cups vegetable stock
1½ cups uncooked couscous

🕐 Prep time: 25 minutes

1 | Knead together butter and flour to form a smooth mixture and place in the freezer.

2 | Peel carrots and finely chop onion, carrots, and zucchini.

3 | In a saucepan, heat oil and braise onion, carrots, and zucchini. Add vegetable juice and bring to a boil. Stir flour-butter mixture bit by bit into the sauce. Simmer for another 5 minutes until it thickens. Season to taste with salt and pepper and sprinkle with parsley.

4 | For the couscous, bring vegetable stock to a boil. Stir in couscous and let stand for 5 minutes. Before serving, fluff with a fork.

Salmon Ragout with Risi Bisi

SERVES 4

➤ For the rice:
1 tbs butter
1⅓ cups basmati rice
2 cups vegetable stock
1½ cups frozen peas
➤ For the fish and sauce:
2 tsp butter
2 tsp flour
1 lb frozen salmon fillet
2 tbs lemon juice
Salt
1 small onion
1 tsp oil
1¼ cups vegetable stock
½ cup cream
Freshly ground pepper
Sugar
1 tsp mustard
1 bunch chopped dill
Hot cooked rice

🕐 Prep time: 30 minutes

1 | In a saucepan, heat butter and sauté rice briefly. Add stock and bring to a boil. Cover and reduce heat. Simmer covered for 15 minutes or until rice is cooked. Stir in peas.

2 | Meanwhile, make the sauce: Knead together butter and flour to form a smooth mixture and place in the freezer. Rinse salmon fillet under cold water, pat dry, and cut into 1-inch cubes. Drizzle with lemon juice and salt lightly.

3 | Finely dice onion. In a saucepan, heat oil and braise onion until translucent. Add stock and cream and bring to a boil. Add flour-butter mixture and stir into sauce with a wire whisk. Simmer sauce until it thickens.

4 | Season sauce to taste with salt, pepper, 1 pinch sugar, mustard, and lemon juice. Add salmon and cook gently for 3–4 minutes until done. Just before serving, add dill. Serve with rice.

◀ *Photo top:* **Vegetable Sauce with Couscous** *Photo bottom:* **Salmon Ragout with Risi Bisi**

Vegetarian

Broccoli Cheese Sauce with Bulgur

SERVES 4

➤ 1 tsp butter
1½ cups bulgur
Salt
1½ lb broccoli
2 slices stale bread
1 tbs oil
⅔ cup milk
3–4 oz soft herb cream cheese
Freshly ground pepper

🕐 Prep time: 35 minutes

1 | In a saucepan, heat butter and braise bulgur briefly. Add 2 cups water and salt and bring to a boil. Cover and simmer over low heat for 30 minutes.

2 | Meanwhile, make the sauce: Rinse broccoli and cut florets from stem. Slice stems thinly and finely chop.

3 | Remove crust from bread and cut into cubes. In a saucepan, heat oil and braise broccoli stems until translucent. Add 2 cups water, stir in milk and cream cheese, and bring to a boil. Purée sauce until smooth and season to taste with salt and pepper.

4 | Add broccoli florets and simmer over low heat for 8 minutes. Fluff bulgur with a fork and serve with broccoli sauce.

Creamed Turkey with Couscous

SERVES 4

➤ 4 turkey cutlets (5 oz each)
Salt
Freshly ground pepper
2 tbs oil
1 small onion
3 slices stale white bread
1 tsp butter
1¾ cups chicken stock
⅔ cup heavy cream
1 tbs chopped chives
2 cups tomato juice
1½ cups uncooked couscous

🕐 Prep time: 30 minutes

1 | Rinse turkey cutlets under cold water and pat dry. Cut into strips and season with salt and pepper.

2 | In a pan, heat oil and brown turkey on both sides for 4 minutes. Remove from pan and set aside.

3 | For the sauce, peel onion and finely dice. Remove crust from bread and finely dice. In a tall saucepan, heat butter and briefly brown onion and bread. Add chicken stock and cream and bring to a boil. Remove from heat and purée. Season to taste with salt and pepper.

4 | For the couscous, bring tomato juice to a boil. Remove from heat, stir in couscous, cover, and let stand for 5 minutes.

5 | Briefly heat turkey in the sauce. Sprinkle sauce with chives. Fluff couscous with a fork and serve with creamed turkey.

Photo top: **Broccoli Cheese Sauce with Bulgur**   *Photo bottom:* **Creamed Turkey with Couscous** ➤

Inexpensive | Classic

Mashed Potatoes

SERVES 4

➤ 2¼ lb russet potatoes
Salt
1¼ cups low-fat milk
2 tbs butter
Freshly ground pepper
Freshly grated nutmeg

🕐 Prep time: 30 minutes

1 | Rinse potatoes. Place in a little salted water and boil in the peels for 20 minutes until tender. Let cool slightly and peel.

2 | Heat milk and butter. Put potatoes through a ricer and add to the milk, or mash in milk with a potato masher. Season with salt, pepper, and a little nutmeg.

➤ Variation: Instead of milk, make purée with buttermilk, tomato juice or vegetable stock, or replace up to half the potatoes with vegetables such as carrots, celery, or peas.

Children's Favorite

Oven Potatoes

SERVES 4

➤ 2 tbs olive oil
½ tsp salt
2¼ lb thin-skinned potatoes
2 tsp dried rosemary, crushed

🕐 Prep time: 15 minutes
🕐 Baking time: 30–45 minutes

1 | Preheat oven to 400°F. Brush oil onto a baking sheet and sprinkle with salt.

2 | Thoroughly scrub potatoes in water with a brush. Cut into quarters. Rub cut edges of potato wedges onto the greased baking sheet and distribute evenly.

3 | Sprinkle potatoes with rosemary. Bake in the oven (middle rack) for 30–45 minutes (depending on their size) until crispy.

Low-fat

Bouillon Potatoes

SERVES 4

➤ 7–8 oz russet potatoes
4 carrots
3–4 oz celery root
1 small leek
1 tbs oil
Soy sauce
1 bunch parsley

🕐 Prep time: 45 minutes

1 | Rinse potatoes, carrots and celery, peel, and cut into ½-inch cubes. Rinse leek, clean, and cut into rings.

2 | In a saucepan, heat oil and brown vegetables. Add potatoes and 1 cup water. Season with a little soy sauce, cover, and simmer for 25–30 minutes until the potatoes are done.

3 | Rinse parsley, shake dry, and finely chop. Season potatoes to taste, sprinkle with parsley, and serve.

All in One

We've taken the best of Italian, Chinese, and Grandma's Cooking: Soup and risotto, stir-fry, casseroles, and pizza and, of course, all types of delicious noodles. Everything is super-fast, simple, and appeals to children and adults, too!

Quick Recipes

Quick Tomato Soup

SERVES 4

➤ 1 onion | 1 clove garlic | 1 tbs olive oil | 3¾ cups tomato juice | ½ cup orange juice | 1 dash balsamic vinegar | 1 tbs dried oregano | Salt | ½ cup grated Parmesan cheese | ⅓ cup low-fat ricotta cheese | ¼ cup bread crumbs | 1 egg | 2 tbs chopped fresh basil | Pepper | Sugar

1 | Peel onion and garlic and finely dice. Heat oil in a medium saucepan and sauté onion and garlic until translucent. Add tomato and orange juices and bring to a boil. Add balsamic vinegar, oregano and ½ tsp salt, and simmer for 10 minutes. Stir together Parmesan, ricotta cheese, bread crumbs, egg, and basil. Shape mixture into small balls and cook gently in the soup for 5 minutes. Season to taste.

Chinese Noodle Soup

SERVES 4

➤ 1 chicken breast (about 4–5 oz) | ½ bunch green onions | 1 tbs oil | 1 lb frozen vegetables (e.g., mixed Asian or soup vegetables) | 4 cups chicken stock | 5 oz crisp noodles (e.g., Chinese egg noodles) | Soy sauce | Pepper

1 | Cut chicken breast into cubes. Rinse onions, clean, and cut into pieces. Heat oil and brown chicken. Add onions and brown briefly. Then add vegetables. Pour in stock and bring to a boil.

1 | Simmer soup over low heat for 5–10 minutes. Simmer noodles in soup until done. Season to taste with soy sauce and pepper.

37

Inexpensive | Easy
Barley Risotto

SERVES 4

➤ 1 onion
1 clove garlic
1/2 cup diced ham
1 1/2 cups pearl barley
4 cups vegetable stock
1 1/2 cups frozen peas
Salt
Freshly ground pepper
1/2 bunch parsley
1 tbs crème fraîche

🕐 Prep time: 40 minutes

1 | Peel onion and garlic, and finely chop onion and mince garlic. In a saucepan, brown ham over medium heat for 2 minutes.

2 | Add onion and garlic and sauté until translucent. Sprinkle in barley and braise briefly until the grains become translucent. Add stock and bring to a boil.

3 | Cover pan and simmer over low heat, stirring frequently, adding more water as necessary. After 20 minutes,

stir in peas and simmer for another 5 minutes, or until barley and peas are cooked.

4 | Rinse parsley, shake dry, and chop finely. Stir parsley and crème fraîche into risotto and season to taste with salt and pepper.

Mediterranean | Easy
Bean Risotto

SERVES 4

➤ 1 onion
1 clove garlic
1 lb runner beans
2 tbs olive oil
1 1/2 cups risotto rice
3 1/3 cups vegetable stock
1 bunch savory
1/2 tsp grated lemon peel
Salt
Freshly ground pepper
1/2 cup freshly grated Parmesan

🕐 Prep time: 35 minutes

1 | Peel onion and garlic and dice finely. Rinse beans, clean, and cut on an angle into 1/2-inch pieces.

2 | In a saucepan, heat oil and braise onion and garlic. Add rice and braise while stirring until the grains become translucent. Add vegetable stock.

3 | Add savory and lemon peel. Simmer risotto over low heat for 10 minutes, stirring frequently.

4 | After cooking for 10 minutes, add beans and simmer risotto for another 10–15 minutes. Season to taste with salt and pepper. Serve sprinkled with Parmesan.

➤ Variation: To make Corn Risotto, replace beans with 2 ears of corn. With a large knife, cut corn from the cobs and braise with rice. In this case, leave out the lemon peel.

Asian
Fried Rice

SERVES 4

➤ 1 cup rice
- 1 bunch green onions
- 2 red bell peppers
- $\frac{1}{2}$ Chinese cabbage
- $\frac{1}{4}$ lb mung bean sprouts
- 1 walnut-sized piece of fresh ginger
- $1\frac{1}{2}$ tbs oil
- 3 tbs soy sauce
- Freshly ground pepper
- $\frac{3}{4}$ lb small, cleaned shrimp

🕓 Prep time: 30 minutes

1 | Prepare rice according to package directions. Rinse vegetables. Clean green onions, dice white parts very finely, and cut green parts into 1-inch pieces. Clean bell peppers and cut into quarters. Cut quarters crosswise into strips. Rinse cabbage and cut into narrow strips. Peel ginger and finely chop.

2 | In a tall pan or wok, heat oil. Stir-fry bell peppers and ginger for 5 minutes. Add green onions and cabbage and stir-fry for another 3 minutes. Finally, add bean sprouts and fry briefly.

3 | Season vegetables with soy sauce and pepper. Add cooked rice and stir well. Continue stir-frying until the rice is hot. Finally, add shrimp and heat only briefly.

➤ Variation: If your child doesn't like shrimp, brown half pound ground beef before preparing the vegetables.

➤ You can make this stir-fry slightly sweet-and-sour by adding 1 small can of drained pineapple chunks.

Vegetarian
Potato Cabbage Hash Browns

SERVES 4

➤ $1\frac{1}{2}$ lb potatoes
- 1 lb cabbage
- 2 eggs
- 2 tbs sour cream
- 2 tbs oil
- Salt
- Freshly ground pepper

🕓 Prep time: 35 minutes
🕓 Baking time: 25–30 minutes

1 | Rinse potatoes and boil in a little water for 10 minutes until half done. Preheat oven to 450°F.

2 | Rinse cabbage, cut out core, and cut into strips. Peel potatoes and coarsely grate.

3 | Place eggs, sour cream and oil in a screw-top jar, seal tightly, and shake vigorously until all the ingredients are mixed together.

4 | In a large bowl, mix grated potatoes and cabbage with the egg mixture and season with salt and pepper.

5 | Line your oven's broiler pan with parchment paper and distribute potato-cabbage mixture evenly on top. Bake in the oven on the middle rack for 25–30 minutes.

➤ Goes with: Tomato Red Pepper Dip or Chive Dip (see page 23).

Rich in Iron
Green Ground Beef Sauce

SERVES 4
- ➤ 1 lb baby spinach
- 1 onion
- 1 clove garlic
- 1 tsp oil
- ½ lb lean ground beef
- Salt
- Freshly ground pepper
- 2 tbs crème fraîche
- ¼ cup heavy cream
- Freshly grated nutmeg

⏱ Prep time: 30 minutes

1 | Rinse spinach, clean, and tear into coarse pieces. Peel onion and garlic and finely chop.

2 | In a large pan, heat oil and braise onion and garlic until translucent. Add ground meat and brown and keep breaking apart with a spoon to make it crumbly. Season with salt and pepper.

3 | Add spinach to meat. Cover and wilt over low heat for 3 minutes.

4 | Stir crème fraîche and cream into the sauce and season to taste with salt, pepper, and 1 pinch nutmeg. Goes best with noodles.

➤ Variation: Instead of spinach, you can use Swiss chard, Chinese cabbage, or bok choy (a type of Chinese cabbage).

TIP It goes faster with frozen spinach.

Fast | Inexpensive
Summer Noodles

SERVES 4
- ➤ 1 lb rotelli pasta
- Salt
- 1 lb ripe tomatoes
- 1 zucchini
- 1 clove garlic
- 3 tbs olive oil
- 2 tbs chopped basil
- Freshly ground pepper
- Freshly grated Parmesan (optional)

⏱ Prep time: 20 minutes

1 | Cook pasta in a large amount of salted water, according to package directions until al dente.

2 | Meanwhile, rinse tomatoes and cut into quarters. Remove seeds and cores and finely dice. Rinse zucchini, clean, and grate finely with a grater. In a large bowl, mix tomatoes and zucchini.

3 | Peel garlic, squeeze through a press, and add to vegetables. Add olive oil and basil. Mix thoroughly and season to taste with salt and pepper.

4 | Drain pasta and stir into vegetables while still hot. Serve immediately. If you want, top with a little freshly grated Parmesan.

➤ Note: Because the tomatoes are raw, they're full of vitamin C.

TIP This recipe stands or falls on the quality of the tomatoes. Use only fully ripe, aromatic tomatoes.

Photo top: **Green Ground Beef Sauce** *Photo bottom:* **Summer Noodles** ➤

Classic
Mushroom Meat Strips

SERANS 4

➤ 1 lb pork cutlets

2 tbs flour

Salt

Pepper

1 tsp paprika

1 onion

¾ lb mushrooms

1½ tbs oil

1¾ cups beef or chicken stock

2 tbs lemon juice

4 tbs cream

🕐 Prep time: 45 minutes

1 | Cut pork into ½-inch wide strips.

2 | Combine flour, 1 tsp salt, a little pepper, and 1 tsp paprika in a freezer bag and mix. Add meat and shake vigorously until the meat is completely coated with flour.

3 | Peel onion and finely dice. Wipe mushrooms with a brush or cloth and thinly slice. In a pan, heat oil and braise onion until translucent. Add meat and brown on all sides over high heat.

4 | Add mushrooms and sear for 3 minutes. Pour in stock and simmer gently for 10 minutes.

5 | Finally, season to taste with lemon juice, salt and pepper, and stir in cream.

➤ Goes with rice, ribbon pasta, or boiled potatoes.

➤ Variation: Instead of pork, use veal, chicken cutlets, or turkey cutlets.

Aromatic
Lamb Stew with Bell Peppers

SERVES 4

➤ 1 lb lamb stew meat

2 onions

1 clove garlic

2 red bell peppers

2 yellow bell peppers

2 tbs oil

2 tbs purchased red pepper tapenade

3 sprigs thyme (may substitute 1 tsp dried thyme)

Salt

Pepper

Sugar

Hungarian sweet paprika

🕐 Prep time: 1 hour and 30 minutes

1 | Rinse lamb under cold water, then pat dry. Peel onions and garlic and finely chop. Rinse bell peppers, clean, and cut into strips.

2 | In a roasting pan, heat oil and braise onions and garlic until translucent. Add meat and sear on all sides. Add bell pepper strips and sauté for 3 minutes.

3 | Stir in tapenade and then add ½ cup water. Add thyme sprigs, cover, and stew over low heat for 1 hour, stirring occasionally and adding liquid if necessary. Season to taste with salt, pepper, sugar, and paprika.

➤ Goes with rice or small, wheat noodles like orzo.

Favorite Recipe
Colorful Pizza

MAKES 1 BAKING SHEET

➤ 1 cup low-fat
  ricotta cheese
  6 tbs oil
  1 egg yolk
  1 tsp salt
  2½ cups all-purpose flour
  1 tbs baking powder
  4 tbs milk (as needed)
  ¼ cup tomato paste
  2 tbs sour cream
  Freshly ground pepper
  2 tsp dried oregano
  1 lb fresh mozzarella cheese
  1 red bell pepper
  1 zucchini
  8 slices deli turkey breast
  Grease for the baking sheet
  Flour for the work surface

🕓 Prep time: 35 minutes
🕓 Baking time: 25 minutes

1 | For the dough: Knead together ricotta cheese, oil, egg yolk, salt, and half the flour. Combine remaining flour with baking powder and knead into dough. If the dough is too firm, add milk one spoonful at a time. With floured hands, knead dough thoroughly until smooth.

2 | Grease a baking sheet. Roll out dough, transfer to the baking sheet, and spread to the edges. Preheat oven to 400°F.

3 | Stir together tomato paste and sour cream until smooth, season with pepper and oregano, and spread evenly over the dough.

4 | Rinse bell pepper, clean, and cut into fine strips. Rinse zucchini, clean, and thinly slice. Drain mozzarella and slice. Top pizza evenly with mozzarella slices and then bell pepper and zucchini (turkey breast comes later on).

5 | Bake pizza in the oven on the bottom rack for 25 minutes. Cut turkey into fine strips. When the pizza is almost done, top with turkey and finish baking.

Fast | Simple
Feta with Vegetables

SERVES 4

➤ 2 small zucchini
  1 eggplant
  1 yellow bell pepper
  2 cups cherry tomatoes
  1 tbs olive oil
  1 tsp dried thyme
  10 oz piece feta cheese
  1 tsp powdered sugar

🕓 Prep time: 20 minutes
🕓 Baking time: 15 minutes

1 | Preheat oven to 475°F. Cover a baking sheet with aluminum foil all the way to the edges.

2 | Rinse zucchini and eggplant and slice. Rinse bell pepper and cut into narrow strips. Rinse tomatoes. Toss vegetables with oil and thyme.

3 | Place feta in the center of the baking sheet and distribute vegetables all around. Dust feta with powdered sugar. Bake in the oven on the second rack from the top for 15 minutes. Serve warm with bread.

Photo top: **Colorful Pizza**   Photo bottom: **Feta with Vegetables** ➤

Healthy Desserts

Here you can let your children help themselves with a clear conscience, thanks to grains and fruit, dairy products, and moderate amounts of sugar. In addition to the classics, there's Apricot Couscous, Chocolate Pancakes, Carrot Muffins, and a basic recipe for a favorite cake.

Quick Recipes

Orange Couscous

SERVES 4

➤ 1 orange | 1 cup orange juice | ¾ cup precooked couscous | ½ cup heavy cream | Cinnamon for garnish

1 | Peel orange and cut into pieces. Stir orange pieces and juice into couscous and let stand for 5 minutes.

2 | Whip cream until stiff. Briefly stir couscous and fold in whipped cream. Serve dusted with a little cinnamon.

➤ Variation: In the summer, replace orange with ¾ lb fresh pitted apricots cut into fine wedges and stir into couscous.

Pudding with Berry Sauce

SERVES 4

➤ 4 cups milk | 1 pinch salt | ½ cup whole-wheat semolina | ¼ cup sugar | ¾ lb mixed berries (fresh or frozen) | Sugar to taste | 3 tbs chopped almonds

1 | Bring milk and salt to a boil. Stir in semolina with a wire whisk. Bring to a boil and cook gently over low heat for 5 minutes while stirring constantly. Then stir in sugar.

2 | For the sauce, rinse berries and sort or thaw and then purée. If desired, put through a strainer. Sweeten with sugar if desired.

Classic with a Twist
Baked Apple Pancake

SERVES 4

➤ 1²⁄₃ cups all-purpose flour
   3 eggs
   Salt
   1 cup milk
   1 dash mineral water
   5 tart apples
   3 tbs sugar
   1 tsp cinnamon

🕑 Prep time: 20 minutes
🕑 Baking time: 15 minutes

1 | Preheat oven to 475°F. Line your oven's broiler pan with parchment paper and heat in the oven.

2 | Whisk together flour, eggs, 1 pinch salt, milk, and mineral water to make a pancake batter.

3 | Rinse apples, peel, cut into quarters, and remove cores. Cut apples into ½-inch thick wedges. Combine sugar and cinnamon.

4 | Evenly spread pancake batter onto the broiler pan.

Top with apple wedges, sprinkle with cinnamon sugar, and bake in the oven (middle rack) for 10–15 minutes until golden-brown.

> **TIP** Instead of apples, top pancake with ripe pears, cherries, plums or apricots, and serve.
>
> Serve with whipped cream or 1 scoop vanilla ice cream.

Chocolate Banana Pancake

SERVES 4

➤ 2 ripe bananas
   1¼ cups all-purpose flour
   1 tbs cocoa powder
   4 eggs
   2 tbs sugar
   1 cup milk
   1 pinch salt
   1 tbs oil
   Powdered sugar

🕑 Prep time: 40 minutes

1 | Mash bananas with a fork. Combine flour and cocoa. Separate eggs. Using a hand mixer, beat egg yolks, sugar, and milk. Gradually add flour-cocoa mixture and stir in bananas.

2 | Beat egg whites with 1 pinch salt until stiff. Carefully fold egg whites into the batter.

3 | In a large pan, heat oil. Pour in half the batter and fry over low heat for 5 minutes until golden-brown. Turn and fry briefly. Using two forks, shred pancake until brown on all sides. Serve dusted with powdered sugar. Repeat procedure with remaining batter.

➤ Variation: Combine banana slices with honey and brown in a pan. Leave out cocoa and sugar; otherwise, prepare as described.

> **TIP** To make a lighter batter, let stand for 30 minutes before folding in the egg whites.

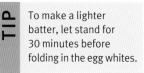

Sophisticated Use
of Leftovers

Black Forest Cherry Pudding

SERVES 4

➤ 1 jar morello cherries
  (about 12½ oz
  drained weight)

6 slices stale
dark pumpernickel

2 tbs cocoa

2 tbs grated chocolate

¼ cup chopped walnuts

2 eggs

1 pinch salt

2 cups low-fat
ricotta cheese

½ cup sugar

6 tbs mineral water

½ tsp vanilla extract

Cocoa powder and
powdered sugar (optional)

🕐 Prep time: 25 minutes
🕐 Baking time: 45 minutes

1 | Preheat oven to 350°F.
Drain cherries in a colander.
Crumble bread. Combine
cocoa, grated chocolate,
and walnuts.

2 | Separate eggs. Beat egg
whites with 1 pinch salt until
stiff. Using a hand mixer
with a whisk attachment,
thoroughly mix egg yolks,
ricotta, sugar, mineral
water, and vanilla. Fold in
egg whites.

3 | Distribute crumbled
bread in a shallow casserole
dish. Spoon ricotta mixture
on top and place cherries in
the mixture.

4 | Bake in the oven (middle
shelf) for 45 minutes. If the
pudding turns too brown,
cover with aluminum foil.
If desired, dust with a little
cocoa powder or powdered
sugar just before serving.

➤ Variation: In the summer,
  you can also use fresh
  pitted cherries, blackberries,
  or currants. Frozen fruit
  also works; place it on the
  ricotta mixture unthawed.

TIP If the bread is very dry,
stir a little milk into the
ricotta cheese mixture.

Rich in Calcium

Sweet Cheese Dumplings

SERVES 4

➤ 3 eggs
  ¼ cup sugar
  2 cups low-fat
  ricotta cheese
  1 cup farina or plain
  cream of wheat
  1¾ cups milk
  1 tbs sugar
  1 pinch salt
  ½ tsp vanilla extract

🕐 Prep time: 20 minutes
🕐 Baking time: 45 minutes

1 | Preheat oven to 350°F.
Combine eggs and sugar
and stir in ricotta and farina
or cream of wheat.

2 | Bring milk, salt and
vanilla to a boil, and pour
into a casserole dish. Use two
moistened tablespoons to
make small dumplings from
ricotta mixture and place
them in the milk mixture.

3 | Cover casserole with
aluminum foil and bake in
the oven (middle rack) for
30 minutes. Remove foil and
bake for another 15 minutes
until the dumplings are
golden-brown.

➤ Goes with: Fruit salad
  or compote.

Photo top: **Black Forest Cherry Pudding**   *Photo bottom:* **Sweet Cheese Dumplings** ➤

For a Child's Party
Batter Cake

MAKES 1 LOAF PAN
(ABOUT 9" X 5")

➤ $3/4$ cup softened butter
($1^1/2$ sticks)

1 pinch salt

$3/4$ cup sugar

$1/2$ tsp vanilla extract

4 eggs

$2/3$ cup milk

2 cups all-purpose flour

2 tsp baking powder

Butter and bread crumbs
for the pan

🕐 Prep time: 30 minutes
🕐 Baking time: 1 hour

1 | Preheat oven to 350°F. Using an electric mixer, beat butter until fluffy. Slowly add sugar and vanilla and continue beating for 5 minutes. Add eggs and mix well. Add milk.

2 | Combine flour and baking powder and stir into the egg mixture with a wooden spoon (not the hand mixer!) to form a smooth thick batter.

3 | Grease bread pan and sprinkle with bread crumbs. Pour in batter and bake in the oven (middle rack) for 1 hour. After 25 minutes, cover with aluminum foil.

4 | After baking for 1 hour, pierce cake with a wooden pick. The pick should come out clean. Let cake cool slightly in the pan and then remove and let cool on a cooling rack.

➤ Variations:

Marble Cake: Stir 6 tbs cocoa powder into half the batter. Layer two types of batter in the pan and swirl with a fork to create a marbled effect.

Citrus Cake: Instead of milk, stir in peel and juice from 2 lemons. Pierce cake several times while still warm and drizzle with the juice of 2–3 oranges and 1 lemon. Glaze with powdered sugar.

Nut Cake: Replace $1^1/2$ cups flour with ground nuts and stir in 2 tsp cocoa powder and $1/3$ cup grated chocolate to recipe.

Chocolate Cake: Add $1/4$ cup cocoa powder, 1 cup grated chocolate, and $1/2$ tsp cinnamon to the batter.

Easy
Vanilla Carrot Muffins

MAKES 12 MUFFINS

➤ $1/2$ lb carrots

2 cups all-purpose flour

2 tsp baking powder

$1/4$ tsp baking soda

$1/4$ tsp salt

$1/4$ tsp cinnamon

2 eggs

$1/2$ cup sugar

$1/2$ cup butter
(1 stick), melted

1 cup vanilla yogurt

$1/4$ cup chopped almonds

12 paper baking cups

🕐 Prep time: 30 minutes
🕐 Baking time: 30 minutes

1 | Preheat oven to 375°F. Line a muffin pan with paper baking cups. Peel carrots and finely grate. Combine all dry ingredients together.

2 | Whisk together eggs, sugar, butter, and vanilla yogurt. Quickly stir in flour mixture. Finally, fold in grated carrots.

3 | Spoon batter into baking cups and sprinkle with almonds. Bake in the oven (middle rack) for 30 minutes.

Photo top: **Batter Cake** *Photo bottom:* **Vanilla Carrot Muffins** ➤

When Your Child is Sick

Diarrhea and Vomiting

What helps
➤ Lots of liquids: Black or peppermint tea and bottled water.
➤ For vomiting: 2–3 hours fasting followed by tea, then plain crackers, or toast.
➤ To stop diarrhea: Peeled and grated apple, mashed banana, plain crackers, or toast.
➤ If your child can keep down tea and plain crackers, give light foods: Mashed potatoes and/or carrots, and plain rice or oatmeal.

What doesn't help
➤ Foods that are fatty, gas-forming, or hard to digest (such as fried foods, legumes, onions, and whole-grain foods).
➤ Purgative foods (such as raw vegetables, applesauce, and yogurt).
➤ Highly acidic foods (such as carbonated beverages, fruit juices, or sour fruits).

Recipe
Tummy Comfort: Brew up 1 tsp fennel seeds, 1 tsp anise seeds and 1 tsp black or peppermint tea in 1 quart boiling water, and steep for 8 minutes. Add 1 pinch salt, 3 tbs fructose, and the juice of 1 lemon.
Gentle Purée: Makes 2 child's servings: Rinse $1/2$ lb russet potatoes, peel, and cut into quarters. Place in $1/2$ cup water with $1/2$ tsp salt and boil for 20 minutes. Peel 4 oz carrots, finely chop, and boil with potatoes for the last 10 minutes. Mash with a potato masher.

Fever

What helps
➤ Lots of liquids, especially after sweating profusely: Ice or lemon water, fruit juices, and tea (lime blossoms promote perspiration).
➤ Cut-up fruit or vegetables, puréed fruit, or noodle bouillon.
➤ Don't force children to eat if they have no appetite.

What doesn't help
➤ The body fights off illness. Food tends to interfere with this.
➤ Hard to digest, fatty, protein-rich dishes, or non-nutritive foods such as sweets and fast food.
➤ Stale or warmed up food.

Recipe
Consommé: Makes 4 servings: Rinse 1 bunch soup greens (e.g., carrot, celery stalk with leaves, celery root, parsnip, parsley root, leek, onion, and parsley), clean, chop finely, and braise in 1 tbs oil. Add 6 cups chicken stock. Simmer gently for 10 minutes. Add $1 1/2$ cups frozen peas and simmer for 6–8 minutes. Cook soup noodles (1–2 oz per serving) in the soup a short time before serving and season to taste with soy sauce and parsley.
Magic Potion: Peel 1 walnut-sized piece of ginger and chop finely. Pour on $1 3/4$ cups boiling water and let stand for 10 minutes. Strain out ginger and combine tea with the juice of 1 orange and 1 tbs honey.

Cold

What works
➤ New studies show: Lots of liquids don't help a lot, so don't force your child to drink! However, liquids do help some and loosen thick mucous.
➤ Helpful herbs and spices (in food or tea): Rosehips, chamomile, peppermint, sage (for coughs), thyme, ginger, mustard, horseradish, and chives.
➤ If the child has trouble swallowing: Sherbet, frozen berries for sucking on.

What doesn't help
➤ Hard, dry dishes that are difficult to chew and swallow.
➤ Empty calories from processed foods, sweets, or soft drinks.

Recipe
Sore Throat Shake: Makes 1 glass: Purée 1 cup fresh or frozen raspberries, 1 small scoop vanilla ice cream, and $2/3$ cup buttermilk. Serve in a tall glass with a straw.
Cream of Broccoli Soup: Makes 4 servings: Rinse 1 small bunch broccoli. Separate into florets. Peel stems and finely chop. Dice 1 onion and braise in 1 tbs oil. Add broccoli stems and braise briefly, then pour in $3\frac{1}{4}$ cups vegetable stock. Bring to a boil and simmer for 5 minutes. Add broccoli florets and simmer for 6–8 minutes. Add $1/2$ cup heavy cream and 1 tbs grated horseradish. Purée and season with salt and pepper.

Recovering from Illness

What helps
➤ Fresh food that is rich in nutrients but easy to digest: Fruit, vegetables, or nuts.
➤ Protein-rich foods: Yogurts, lean meat, or fish.
➤ Indulge their whims, make everything look appetizing; offer several small meals throughout the day.

What doesn't help
➤ Confectionery, snack foods, soft drinks, fast food, which are all high in calories but provide too few valuable nutrients.
➤ Foods hard to digest such as fried and fatty foods.

Recipe
Risotto Bolognese: Makes 2 servings: Dice 1 onion and 1 clove garlic and braise in 1 tsp oil. Brown 5–6 oz ground lean beef and season with salt and pepper. Add $3/4$ cup risotto rice, 2 cups tomato juice, 1 cup water, and 1 medium bell pepper, diced. Simmer for 20 minutes. Season with salt, pepper, and 3 tbs chopped basil. Serve with Parmesan.
Crunchy Yogurt: Makes 1 serving: Purée $1/2$ cup yogurt, $1/4$ cup orange juice, and 1 banana. In an ungreased pan, toast 2 tbs each of chopped walnuts, pumpkin seeds, and oat flakes. Sprinkle over yogurt and dust with a little cinnamon.

If My Child...

...Can't Tolerate Milk

An inability to tolerate cow's milk often occurs during the first years of life, and usually disappears after ½ to 1 year. It would be a mistake to permanently ban milk from your child's diet in response to the least little problem. If it's lactose that your child can't tolerate, they can usually eat yogurt and cheese. If the problem is milk protein, however, you'll have to change to soy products. Make sure it's enriched with calcium (at least 100 mg per 3.5 oz) because otherwise your child will store too little calcium in their bones. They need about 2 cups milk or 1½ cups yogurt or even 2 oz firm cheese per day. If choosing bottled water, make sure you select calcium-rich mineral water. Read the list of ingredients before purchasing prepared products. Milk protein and lactose can be hidden, for example, in baked goods, bread, instant soups, hot dogs, confectionery, pasta, and frozen dishes.

...Can't Tolerate Eggs

It isn't easy to cook and bake without eggs but it is possible. It's more difficult to find egg-free commercial baked goods, confectionery, prepared product, and dressings. Sometimes even clear juices contain residues from egg whites that were used to clarify them. Health food stores will be able to supply a complete list of egg-free products.

...Can't Tolerate Wheat

Children with an actual coeliac disease can't eat gluten. Gluten is present in wheat, spelt, barley, spelt, oats, and rye. Only corn, millet, and buckwheat are gluten-free, but baking must be done without yeast or sourdough. The only possible leavening agent is baking powder. The lack of a stabilizing capacity in these flours for pancakes, etc., can be compensated for by adding more eggs. Health food stores offer a wide range of gluten-free products. If your child has only a mild intolerance, it's often sufficient to replace wheat with spelt. The other grain varieties are better tolerated. Overall, whole-wheat is better tolerated than white flour.

...If Vegetarian

As long as your child still consumes milk, dairy products and, perhaps, eggs and fish, they're sure to get enough protein. Whole wheat, nuts, seeds, mushrooms, and legumes (including soy) supply valuable plant protein. However, they may not be getting enough iron, which is important for oxygenation. To take care of the problem, give them food rich in whole grains (especially millet) and seeds (especially sesame). It's best to combine them with vitamin-C rich juice or vegetables because this facilitates iron absorption. Also, spinach really is full of iron!

...Has Neurodermitis

There is no clearly effective neurodermitis diet. All you can do is learn what aggravates the disease on a trial-and-error basis. Often it's attributed to processed foods, additives in general, confectionery, sugar, white flour, milk, dairy products, and certain types of fruit. Start with a simple diagnostic diet and gradually introduce individual foods. This is the best way to discover the foods to which your child has a bad reaction.

...Weighs Too Much

The older the overweight child, the lower their chance of achieving a normal body weight. Don't subject kindergarten-age children to a diet, but pay attention if their weight is above the curve for more than 6 months (see page 5). At this age, it's enough to maintain the same weight for several months while growth eats up the extra pounds. But even this is difficult for some children. Eliminate soft drinks and juices. Water and unsweetened teas quench thirst without calories. Choose low-fat (1.5 percent)

milk and dairy products. Make sure their diet is rich in fiber. Choose low-fat lunchmeats and cheese. Serve your child lots of whole grains in the form of granola and bread, and lots of fruit and vegetables. Eliminate between-meal snacking. Above all, make sure your child exercises.

...Weighs Too Little

Avoid sweets and snacking because this will ruin your child's appetite for main meals. Food for overly thin children must be rich in vitamins, minerals, and calories. Dairy products with their natural fat content, healthy oils, nuts, and hard cheese provide energy without filling up their stomach. Despite your concern, avoid entering into power struggles with your child over eating. Eating should not be the number-one issue between mother and child.

...Is Constantly Constipated

Constipation can occur if your child drinks too little, doesn't consume enough fiber, and doesn't get enough exercise.

Also, some children tend to suffer from chronic constipation. If this is the case, talk to your pediatrician. Never give children laxatives because they will damage their intestines and slow them down for good. If nothing else works, use an enema from the pharmacy.

The following gets the bowels moving:
➤ Lots of liquids.
➤ A diet rich in fiber with lots of raw fruit, vegetables, and whole grains.
➤ Pro-biotic yogurts.
➤ Yellow flaxseed and dried plums soaked overnight and served in granola.
➤ 1–2 tsp lactose dissolved in yogurt, applesauce, or milk.

ABBREVIATIONS

lb = pound
oz = ounce
tsp = teaspoon
tbs = tablespoon

The Author

Dagmar von Cramm Dagmar is a nutritionist and lives in Germany. She has written extensively on topics related to children, adolescents, and nutrition. As the mother of three children, she not only bases her lovingly researched and formulated books on her extensive academic experience, but on her very personal family experience as well. She also serves on the board of the German Nutrition Society. As a journalist, she writes for parents' magazines, among other publications. Beyond her activities as an author, Dagmar is known for her work as a moderator and expert on radio and TV.

The Photographer

After completing his studies at a photography school in Berlin, Michael Brauner worked as an assistant to renowned photographers in France and Germany before striking out on his own in 1984. His unique, atmospheric style, coming out of his studio, is highly valued by advertising firms and book publishers around the world.

Photo Credits

Sigrid Reinichs, Munich: cover photo, pages 1, 6, 9, 12 All others: Michael Brauner

Published originally under the title Kochen für Kleinkinder: was Kinder gerne essen © 2004 Gräfe und Unzer Verlag GmbH, Munich. English translation for the U.S. market © 2005, Silverback Books, Inc.

Program director: Doris Birk
Managing editor: Birgit Rademacker, Lisa Tooker (US)
Editor: Susanne Klug, Stefani Poziombka, Rosemary Mart (US)
Reader: Bettina Bartz
Layout, typography and design: Independent Medien Design, Munich
Typesetting: Uhl + Massopust, Aalen
Production: Gloria Pall, Patty Holden (US)
Reproduction: Repro Ludwig, Zell am See

ISBN 1-59637-040-8

Printed in China

Enjoy Other Quick & Easy Books

Coffee and Espresso

Tanja Dusy

Christmas Cookies

1 Pan— 50 Muffins

Preserves and Canning

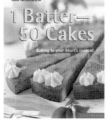

Irresistible Fondue

Angelika Illies

Cooking for Two

Cornelia Adam

Napkins

Fast Italian

Margit Proebst

Andreas Fürtmayr

Sushi

Classic ideas from Japan and new fusion sushi
Home-made perfectly

Gina Greifenstein

1 Batter— 50 Cakes

Baking to your heart's content

Cooking in Clay

Healthy Recipes with Great Flavor

Erika Casparek-Türkkan

1 Noodle, 50 Sauces

Everyday Pasta • Old and New Italian Dishes
Noodle biography • 10 Tips for Success

Antje Gruener

Grilling

Crisp, flavorful and hot vegetable morsels from the
grid for real barbecue food, from spareribs to
skewered vegetables with sauces and chutneys.

Sauces and Dips

Soups

Classic to Contemporary

Sebastian Dickhaut

Claudia Schmidt

Raclette

New Recipes with Cheese Princes and Party Dips

Antipasti and Tapas

Mediterranean Appetizers
Cornelia Schinharl

Cornelia Adam

Garlic

Sophisticated Recipes with the Eastern
Spice of the Mediterranean Region
Spicy (tangy), sour (delicate), international.

Cornelia Adam

Salads

Sandwiches

Xenia Burgtorf

Marlisa Szwillus

Fondue

Cheese, vegetable, all kinds
of meat—everything right at
the table! More than 50 recipes

Cornelia Adam

Quiche

Delicious, savory pies with
vegetables, meat, poultry or
fish—done for all occasions

SUFFICIENT IODINE

- A small percentage of children under the age of 10 have goiters due to iodine deficiency.
- Use iodized salt in your child's food.
- Choose bread, cheese, and meat seasoned with iodized salt.
- Serve seafood once per week.

Guaranteed Perfect Cooking for Children

THE RIGHT FAT

- Children need 25–30 g fat per day.
- Canola oil is ideal because of its fatty acids. Sunflower oil is high in vitamin E.
- Small amounts of butter used as spreadable fat supply vitamin D.
- As much as possible, avoid hidden fats in hot dogs, meat, cheese, baked and processed foods, and confectionery items.

SWEETS IN MODERATION

- Toddlers shouldn't consume more than 2½ tbs of sugar per day; kindergarten-aged children shouldn't consume more than 3 tbs.
- Sweeteners with more nutritional value include honey, concentrated agave juice, whole cane sugar, maple syrup, and concentrated apple juice.
- Children don't need artificial sweeteners or other flavorings.

REGULAR MEAL TIMES

- It's important to have fixed meal times every day, preferably as a family.
- Even the two snacks should be eaten at the table and not as a casual aside.
- Drinking between times is okay, but not munching.